D0895465

Wild Rides!

Sprint Cars

By A. R. Schaefer

Consultant:

Betty Carlan

International Motorsports Hall of Fame

Talladega, Alabama

Capstone press

Mankato, Minnesota

Edge Books are published by Capstone Press
151 Good Counsel Drive, P.O. Box 669, Mankato, Minnesota 56002
www.capstonepress.com

Library of Congress Cataloging-in-Publication Data
Schaefer, A. R. (Adam Richard), 1976–
    Sprint cars / by A. R. Schaefer.
        p. cm.—(Edge books, Wild rides!)
    Includes bibliographical references and index.
    ISBN 0-7368-2727-7 (hardcover)
    1. Sprint cars—Juvenile literature. 2. Automobile racing—Juvenile literature.
[1. Sprint cars. 2. Automobile racing.] I. Title. II. Series.
GV1029.9.S67S33 2005
796.72—dc22   2003027108

Summary: Discusses sprint cars, including their history, design,
    and competitions.

Editorial Credits
Donald Lemke, editor; Kia Adams, series designer; Patrick D. Dentinger,
    book designer; Jo Miller, photo researcher; Eric Kudalis, product
    planning editor

Photo Credits
Artemis Images, cover, 4, 7, 16, 18, 20, 23, 24–25, 27, 28; Indianapolis
    Motor Speedway, 8
Corbis/Hulton-Deutsch Collection, 11
Getty Images/Hulton Archive, 10
Tear-Off Heaven Fotos/Steve Lafond Photo, 13, 14, 19

Table of Contents

Learn about:

- **Pro sprint car racing**

- **Amateur sprint car racing**

- **Prize money**

CHAPTER **1**

Sprint Cars

The sprint cars speed away from the starting line. One car quickly takes the lead. Soon, the lead car reaches the first turn. The driver turns the steering wheel hard to the left. The car's giant back tires spin on the dirt track. They splatter dirt into the stands. The sprint car starts sliding to the right. Finally, the tires catch the ground and gain traction. The car speeds toward the next turn.

After 30 laps, the lead car flies across the finish line. The track official waves the checkered flag. Fans stand and cheer for the winning driver.

Sprint Car Races

Sprint cars come in different shapes and sizes. Each sprint car league has rules about engine size and car design. Some sprint cars have giant wings. Other sprint cars look more like dune buggies.

Pro and amateur sprint car racing is popular in many countries. Thousands of people gather to watch pro sprint car races. Pro races are sometimes shown on TV. The winner of a big race could win $50,000 to $100,000. Amateur sprint car races take place at small racetracks. Winning drivers might only get a $50 prize. Still, hundreds of fans enjoy watching these races from the stands.

Most sprint car drivers race on short dirt
tracks in front of fans.

Learn about:

- **Open-wheel racing**

- **Midget cars**

- **World of Outlaws**

CHAPTER **2**

Early Sprint Cars

In 1894, car racing began in France. Since then, many types of race cars have been built. They include Indy cars, midget cars, and sprint cars. All of these cars have changed over time. They continue to become more advanced racing machines.

First Race Cars

In the early 1900s, open-wheel car racing became popular in the United States. Open-wheel cars do not have fenders to cover the wheels. In 1911, the first Indianapolis 500 took place in Indiana. It was the first major open-wheel race in the United States.

In the 1930s, people built small open-wheel cars called midgets.

By the early 1930s, companies started making small open-wheel race cars. These smaller cars became known as midgets. Midgets cost less money to build than regular-size race cars. More people could afford to enter races.

During the 1940s and 1950s, some drivers started racing on paved tracks. Most small racetracks could not afford to pave over the dirt. Midget drivers continued racing on the dirt tracks. Regular-size cars ran on the paved racetracks. These cars became known as Indy cars.

Sprint Cars

Soon, another type of race car became popular with fans. Sprint cars were smaller than Indy cars but larger than midget cars. Sprint cars were built for both paved and dirt tracks. They could travel very fast in short races.

Wings on Sprint Cars

During the 1960s, some drivers added a giant wing to the roofs of their sprint cars. The wing captured air and pushed down on the car. It gave the car better traction. Wings also made the car safer. If a sprint car flipped over, the wing helped protect the driver.

Winged sprint cars became popular during the 1970s and 1980s. But some traditional sprint car leagues did not allow wings on cars. Some drivers formed their own winged leagues. The World of Outlaws (WoO) Series is one of these leagues. Today, both winged and traditional sprint cars have their own leagues and fans.

Many fans enjoy watching winged sprint car races.

Learn about:

- **Wings**

- **Wheel size**

- **Roll cages**

CHAPTER **3**

Designing a Sprint Car

Each sprint car league has different rules about car design and engine size. But most sprint cars have the same basic features. They are designed to be light, fast, and safe.

Basic Features

The frame of a sprint car is called a chassis. A chassis is usually made of hollow pipes. Hollow pipes are lighter than solid materials. A light car can go faster and accelerate more quickly than a heavy car. But a light car may have problems getting traction around corners.

Many sprint car leagues have rules about the weight of a sprint car. In 2004, cars in the American Sprint Car Series (ASCS) had to weigh at least 1,475 pounds (669 kilograms).

Wings on sprint cars can help drivers gain traction. Winged cars usually have two wings. Some cars have a small wing on the front. This wing is usually 2 feet (.6 meter) wide and 3 feet (.9 meter) long. A larger wing sits on the roof of the car. It is usually 5 feet (1.5 meters) wide

Many winged sprint cars have wings on the front and the roof of the car.

and 5 feet long. Some wings are hooked to hydraulic systems. The driver can move these wings during a race.

Wheels

Sprint car leagues have limits on wheel size. The front wheels are smaller than the rear wheels. In the United States Auto Club (USAC) Series, the front wheels can't be more than 10 inches (25 centimeters) wide. Sometimes, the left rear wheel is smaller than the right rear wheel. In the USAC Series, the left rear wheel can only be 14 inches (36 centimeters) wide. But the right rear wheel can be 18 inches (46 centimeters) wide. The larger wheel helps the car turn left around an oval racetrack.

Engines

Most sprint car leagues also limit engine size. Bigger engines are more powerful and cost more money. The largest engines can power sprint cars to speeds of about 100 miles (160 kilometers) per hour.

Sprint car engines are measured in cubic inches. WoO sprint car drivers use 410-cubic-inch engines. Many other sprint car leagues use 360-cubic-inch engines. Some leagues require even smaller engines.

Seat belts and padding help keep sprint car drivers safe.

Safety Equipment

Sprint cars have several pieces of safety equipment. All sprint cars have seat belts and padding. These items keep drivers from being thrown around during a race. They also protect drivers during a wreck.

Sprint cars have a firewall between the engine and the driver. A firewall slows the spread of an engine fire. It gives the driver time to escape a burning car.

In traditional sprint cars, the hollow pipe frame increases safety. If the car rolls over, the frame works as a roll cage. The roll cage protects the driver's head and neck from injury. In winged cars, the wings also help protect the driver.

Sprint cars have roll cages to protect drivers during a crash.

Learn about:

- **Hot laps**

- **Qualifying**

- **Caution laps**

CHAPTER 4

Sprint Cars in Competition

Most of today's sprint leagues run winged cars. In some areas, traditional sprint cars are still popular. Both kinds of cars make for an exciting race.

Race Organization

Many leagues put on sprint car races. The WoO is the best-known winged league. WoO has races all over the United States. The ASCS and All-Star Circuit of Champions also race winged sprint cars. The Sprint Car Racing Association and the USAC put on traditional sprint car races.

Some racetracks put on their own sprint car races. These races are not part of any official racing league. Local drivers usually race in these events. Their cars have smaller engines and do not cost as much as league cars.

Race Night

Race nights are a little different at each track. Usually, the teams arrive in the afternoon. Before the race starts, each team is allowed to run hot laps. Hot laps are for practice. They give the drivers a chance to test their cars on the racetrack.

After the hot laps, the drivers need to qualify. During qualifying rounds, each driver runs one or two laps. The drivers with the best times advance to the heat races.

Heat races are usually eight to 10 laps long. The fastest drivers from each heat race move on to the feature race.

Sprint car racers practice by driving
hot laps before a race starts.

Feature Race

The feature race is longer than the heat races. It is between 20 and 60 laps. Most sprint cars race on tracks that are less than .5 mile (.8 kilometer) long. The entire race is usually 5 to 30 miles (8 to 48 kilometers) long.

Since sprint races are short, they do not have pit stops. The race cars do not travel far enough to run out of gas. Tires do not get worn down. A car with a mechanical problem is usually out of the race.

Sprint cars start feature races close together.

Caution laps do not count in sprint car racing. Caution laps begin when there has been a wreck or a problem with the track. The race official waves a yellow flag. When drivers see the yellow flag, they need to slow down and watch out. They are not allowed to pass. When the track is clear, the official waves a green flag. The drivers can continue the race.

Sometimes, the official will wave a red flag. This flag stops the race and gives officials time to clean up the track. An official only waves a red flag when track conditions are very bad.

When one lap remains in the race, the track official waves a white flag. The cars race to the finish, and the official waves a checkered flag. The first car over the line wins the race and first prize.

The winner of the feature race receives
first prize.

Steve Kinser

Racing fans know Steve Kinser as the "King." During his career, Kinser has won every major sprint car title. He has won most of them several times. In 1978, Kinser won the first World of Outlaws Series title. Since then, he has won this title 17 more times. In 1987, Kinser set a record for the most wins in one year. He won 56 feature races.

Kinser has been successful at other kinds of racing. In 1994, he won an IROC race at Talladega Superspeedway. In 1997, he finished 14th at the Indianapolis 500.

Kinser continues to be a top sprint car driver. In 2000, he was voted sprint car racing's greatest driver by the National Sprint Car Hall of Fame and Museum. In 2004, the King was still racing and winning at 50 years old.

Glossary

accelerate (ak-SEL-uh-rate)—to gain speed or speed up

amateur (AM-uh-chur)—an athlete who usually does not earn a living from competing in a sport

chassis (CHASS-ee)—the frame on which the body of a vehicle is built

fender (FEN-dur)—a covering over a wheel that protects it from damage

hollow (HOL-oh)—having an empty space inside

hydraulic (hye-DRAW-lik)—creating power by forcing liquid under pressure through pipes

league (LEEG)—a group of people with a common interest or activity, such as a group of sports teams

official (uh-FISH-uhl)—the person who enforces the rules of the race

pit (PIT)—the area of a racetrack where cars go to be refueled and fixed; sprint races don't have pit stops.

traction (TRAK-shuhn)—the friction or gripping power that keeps a sprint car from slipping on a surface

Read More

Fox, Martha Capwell. *Car Racing.* History of Sports. San Diego: Lucent Books, 2004.

Sessler, Peter, and Nilda Sessler. *Sprint Cars.* Off to the Races. Vero Beach, Fla.: Rourke Press, 1999.

Thompson, Luke. *Sprint Car.* Built for Speed. New York: Children's Press, 2001.

Internet Sites

FactHound offers a safe, fun way to find Internet sites related to this book. All of the sites on FactHound have been researched by our staff.

Here's how:

1. Visit *www.facthound.com*

2. Type in this special code **0736827277** for age-appropriate sites. Or enter a search word related to this book for a more general search.

3. Click on the **Fetch It** button.

FactHound will fetch the best sites for you!

Index